THE STORY OF BABE RUTH

HOME·RUN

Robert Burleigh

Illustrated by

Mike Wimmer

VOYAGER BOOKS • HARCOURT, INC.

San Diego   New York   London

He is the Babe.

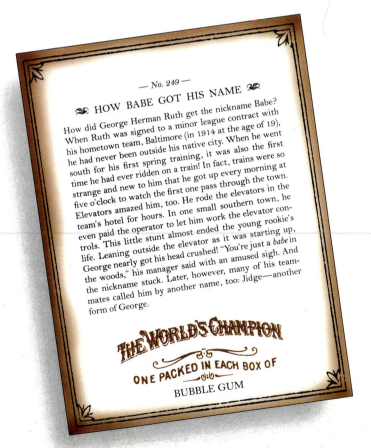

— No. 249 —

❧ HOW BABE GOT HIS NAME ❧

How did George Herman Ruth get the nickname Babe? When Ruth was signed to a minor league contract with his hometown team, Baltimore (in 1914 at the age of 19), he had never been outside his native city. When he went south for his first spring training, it was also the first time he had ever ridden on a train! In fact, trains were so strange and new to him that he got up every morning at five o'clock to watch the first one pass through the town. Elevators amazed him, too. He rode the elevators in the team's hotel for hours. In one small southern town, he even paid the operator to let him work the elevator controls. This little stunt almost ended the young rookie's life. Leaning outside the elevator as it was starting up, George nearly got his head crushed! "You're just a *babe* in the woods," his manager said with an amused sigh. And the nickname stuck. Later, however, many of his teammates called him by another name, too: Jidge—another form of George.

THE WORLD'S CHAMPION

ONE PACKED IN EACH BOX OF

BUBBLE GUM

He has always loved this game.

This baseball.

But what he does not know yet is this:

He will change this game he loves.

Forever.

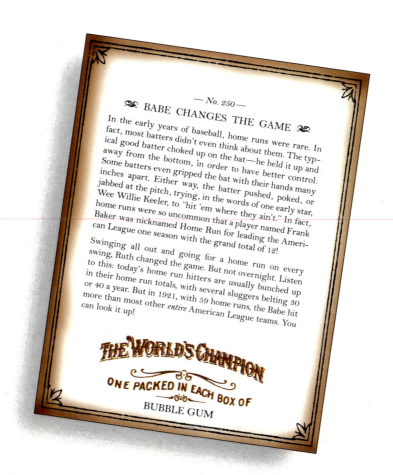

— No. 250 —

☙ BABE CHANGES THE GAME ❧

In the early years of baseball, home runs were rare. In fact, most batters didn't even think about them. The typical good batter choked up on the bat—he held it up and away from the bottom, in order to have better control. Some batters even gripped the bat with their hands many inches apart. Either way, the batter pushed, poked, or jabbed at the pitch, trying, in the words of one early star, Wee Willie Keeler, to "hit 'em where they ain't." In fact, home runs were so uncommon that a player named Frank Baker was nicknamed Home Run for leading the American League one season with the grand total of 12!

Swinging all out and going for a home run on every swing, Ruth changed the game. But not overnight. Listen to this: today's home run hitters are usually bunched up in their home run totals, with several sluggers belting 30 or 40 a year. But in 1921, with 59 home runs, the Babe hit more than most other *entire* American League teams. You can look it up!

THE WORLD'S CHAMPION

ONE PACKED IN EACH BOX OF

BUBBLE GUM

He has always had this swing.
This easy, upthrusting swing.
This "pretty" swing,
not taught by any coach.
One day the Babe just swung—
and it was there.
It was his.

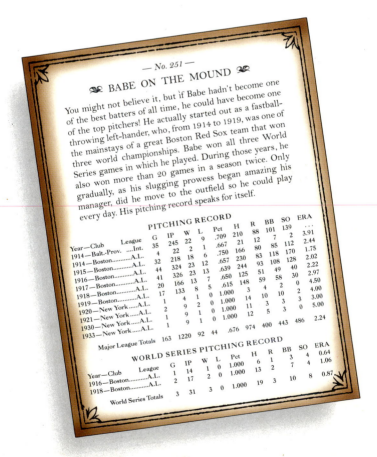

— No. 251 —

❦ BABE ON THE MOUND ❧

You might not believe it, but if Babe hadn't become one of the best batters of all time, he could have become one of the top pitchers! He actually started out as a fastball-throwing left-hander, who, from 1914 to 1919, was one of the mainstays of a great Boston Red Sox team that won three world championships. Babe won all three World Series games in which he played. During those years, he also won more than 20 games in a season twice. Only gradually, as his slugging prowess began amazing his manager, did he move to the outfield so he could play every day. His pitching record speaks for itself.

PITCHING RECORD

Year—Club	League	G	IP	W	L	Pct	H	R	BB	SO	ERA
1914—Balt.-Prov.	Int.	35	245	22	9	.709	210	88	101	139	...
1914—Boston	A.L.	4	22	2	1	.667	21	12	7	2	3.91
1915—Boston	A.L.	32	218	18	6	.750	166	80	85	112	2.44
1916—Boston	A.L.	44	324	23	12	.657	230	83	118	170	1.75
1917—Boston	A.L.	41	326	23	13	.639	244	93	108	128	2.02
1918—Boston	A.L.	20	166	13	7	.650	125	51	49	40	2.22
1919—Boston	A.L.	17	133	8	5	.615	148	59	58	30	2.97
1920—New York	A.L.	1	4	1	0	1.000	3	4	2	0	4.50
1921—New York	A.L.	2	9	2	0	1.000	14	10	10	2	4.00
1930—New York	A.L.	1	9	1	0	1.000	11	3	3	3	3.00
1933—New York	A.L.	1	9	1	0	1.000	12	5	3	0	5.00
Major League Totals		163	1220	92	44	.676	974	400	443	486	2.24

WORLD SERIES PITCHING RECORD

Year—Club	League	G	IP	W	L	Pct	H	R	BB	SO	ERA
1916—Boston	A.L.	1	14	1	0	1.000	6	1	3	4	0.64
1918—Boston	A.L.	2	17	2	0	1.000	13	2	7	4	1.06
World Series Totals		3	31	3	0	1.000	19	3	10	8	0.87

When he misses,

you can hear the bat go *swish*.

He twists round and round.

— *No. 254* —

❧ BABE GOES SWISH! ❧

Did Babe strike out often? Well, yes and no. With a life-time total of 1,330 whiffs, he *did* hold the major league record for strikeouts for many years. (The record was later broken by another Yankee slugger, Reggie Jackson.) But don't be fooled. Ruth wasn't an all-or-nothing kind of hitter, like many players who have followed him. Check this out: his lifetime batting average was .342, good enough to rank him among the highest-average hitters in baseball history! That means he repeatedly made good contact with the ball. His awesome 1923 batting record is a good example.

Year—Club	League	Pos	G	AB	R	H	2B	3B	HR	RBI	BA	PO	A	E	FA
1923—New York	A.L.	OF-1B	152	520	*151	205	45	13	*41	*131	.394	419	21	12	.973

Indicates batter led league in this category

THE WORLD'S CHAMPION

ONE PACKED IN EACH BOX OF

BUBBLE GUM

Even his pop-ups
rise higher than anyone else's.
Skyward.
Higher than the top
of the great stadium.

— No. 255 —

❧ "THAR SHE BLOWS!" ❧

Measuring Babe's longest—as opposed to his highest—hits was a favorite fan pastime. Some of the Sultan of Swat's towering home runs traveled more than 500 feet. One king-size carom was described by an amazed sportswriter like this: "The ball went over the fence, over the street, over the rooftop of another house, atop still another house, and then bounced off down the street two blocks away!" In fact, the Babe's very last major league home run was smacked completely over the double-deck right-field roof of Pittsburgh's old Forbes Field, a feat never before accomplished.

THE WORLD'S CHAMPION

ONE PACKED IN EACH BOX OF

BUBBLE GUM

But sometimes Babe's body
and Babe's bat
and the small white ball
are completely one.

Then it is as it should be.

Smooth as silk.

Easy as air on the face.

Right as falling water.

Then there is only

the echoey, nothing-quite-like-it sound

and soft feel

of the fat part of the bat

on the center of the ball.

— No. 256 —

GETTING THAT FEELING!

When Babe "got the feeling," look out! He didn't slug a homer every time up—but his home run average per times at bat was amazing. Over a twenty-year career, he averaged 1 home run for every 11.7 at bats. And stories of the Babe predicting home runs are part of the Ruthian legend. Babe once promised a sick boy he'd hit him a home run—and he did. Even more famous is Babe's "called shot." It happened (if it did happen) in a 1932 World Series game in Chicago. Some people say he pointed to the center-field stands—and hit the next pitch right there!

THE WORLD'S CHAMPION

ONE PACKED IN EACH BOX OF

BUBBLE GUM

Babe understands this feeling.

He does not know when or where.

But he waits for it.

He wants it.

Again

and again.

— No. 257 —

❧ WHAT WAS BABE'S BEST YEAR? ❧

Many people know that Babe's top home run season was 1927, when he bashed 60 big ones for a record that would stand for more than 30 years. But was that the best season ever for the Goliath of Grand Slam? Some experts think not. Compare two of Ruth's slam-bangingest seasons and judge for yourself.

Year—Club League Pos	G	AB	R	H	2B	3B	HR	RBI	BA	PO	A	E	FA
1921—New York ....A.L. OF-1B-P	152	540	*177	204	44	16	*59	*171	.378	357	19	13	.967
1927—New York ....A.L. OF	151	540	*158	192	29	8	*60	164	.356	328	14	13	.963

*Indicates batter led league in this category

THE WORLD'S CHAMPION

ONE PACKED IN EACH BOX OF

BUBBLE GUM

He watches the pitcher lean.

Rotate.

Rock back and forth.

The leg wheels out.

The arm whips over the head.

Babe narrows his hunter-like gaze

and strides into the pitch

that is now only a tiny speck of whirling whiteness.

This time.

— No. 258 —

❧ BABE ON BATTING ❧

Ruth was far from a baseball philosopher. Once when someone asked him how he hit so many home runs, he simply answered: "I just keep swinging." But, indeed, he thought more than that about hitting a baseball. "I swing as hard as I can," he once said, "and I try to swing right *through* the ball. I always try to follow through. The harder you grip the bat, the more you can swing it through the ball, the farther the ball will go." Babe held his bat at the very end—and then some: he curled his right (lower) hand over the knob, and as the season progressed, he developed a big callus on his palm! All in all, his methods must have worked. When the King of Clout retired in 1935, he held over 40 American League or major league power-hitting records.

THE WORLD'S CHAMPION

ONE PACKED IN EACH BOX OF

BUBBLE GUM

He swings big.

His bat comes down and around.

Powerfully.

He swings "through the ball."

Always "through the ball."

— No. 259 —

JUST STROLLING ALONG—
RECORD-STYLE!

If an opposing pitcher was a bit cautious about throwing to the Babe, he wasn't alone. During his 20-plus years in the majors, Ruth received more than 2,000 bases on balls. In 1923, he received a grand total of 170, setting a major league record. Furthermore, he led the American League in bases on balls for 11 seasons. And think of this: if you include all his walks, the Babe's lifetime on-base percentage was over .500. This means that on average he reached first base—or farther—every other time up!

THE WORLD'S CHAMPION

ONE PACKED IN EACH BOX OF

BUBBLE GUM

There.

There it is.

The feeling that is like no feeling at all!

The ball cracks off the bat.

It soars far up in the air

as it passes first base.

Going, going.

— No. 260 —

"HIGH-LIFE" BABE!

"I swing big—and I live big, too," the Babe once said. And he wasn't kidding! The Bambino loved driving low-slung convertibles, donning silk shirts and coonskin coats, and downing huge meals. A Ruthian breakfast might include a dozen eggs and half a loaf of toast. During games, he would often order a bag of hot dogs to be brought to the Yankee dugout. When he went out on the town, he was a big spender. His tips were famous—sometimes over $100 a pop. Babe liked to stay out late partying, too. Once a reporter asked Ruth's longtime roommate what it was like to live with the Babe. "I can't say much," the man answered. "I didn't really room with Babe. I roomed with his suitcase!"

THE WORLD'S CHAMPION

ONE PACKED IN EACH BOX OF

BUBBLE GUM

The fans crane their necks to follow.

But Babe already knows.

The perfectness.

The feeling.

The boy-fire inside the body of a man.

— No. 261 —

❧ KING BABE! ❧

Whenever he played, Babe Ruth drew in the fans. Even at postseason exhibition games, thousands of people would come out to see the Babe perform. The 1920 Yankees set a one-season attendance record that wasn't broken until 1946. For good reason, Yankee Stadium was called the House That Ruth Built. When the stadium opened in April 1923, more than 60,000 fans jammed into what was then the largest ballpark in America. And rumor has it that many more had to be turned away! The Babe didn't disappoint the spectators, either: he smashed a home run and led the home team to victory.

THE WORLD'S CHAMPION

ONE PACKED IN EACH BOX OF

BUBBLE GUM

He moves down the line.

Slowly.

He squints.

He watches the ball disappear

in a distant blaze of white shirts and blurred faces.

Home run.

Home Run.

Gone.

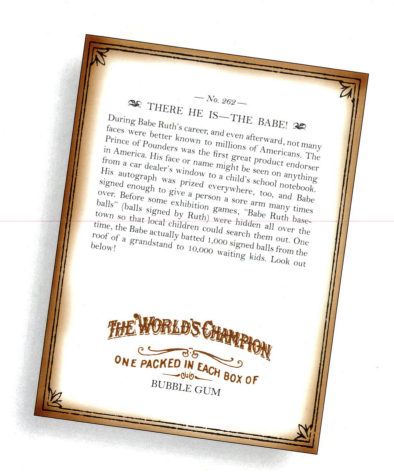

— No. 262 —

❧ THERE HE IS—THE BABE! ❧

During Babe Ruth's career, and even afterward, not many faces were better known to millions of Americans. The Prince of Pounders was the first great product endorser in America. His face or name might be seen on anything from a car dealer's window to a child's school notebook. His autograph was prized everywhere, too, and Babe signed enough to give a person a sore arm many times over. Before some exhibition games, "Babe Ruth baseballs" (balls signed by Ruth) were hidden all over the town so that local children could search them out. One time, the Babe actually batted 1,000 signed balls from the roof of a grandstand to 10,000 waiting kids. Look out below!

THE WORLD'S CHAMPION

ONE PACKED IN EACH BOX OF

BUBBLE GUM

He trots with short steps.

Across the loose dirt of the infield.

Over the soft hardness of the bases

beneath his spiked shoes.

Under the roar of cheering voices

that falls on him like warm rain.

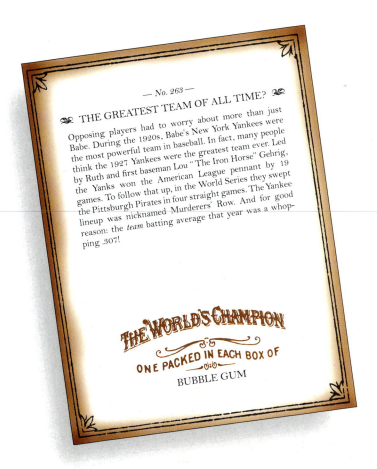

— No. 263 —

🙢 THE GREATEST TEAM OF ALL TIME? 🙠

Opposing players had to worry about more than just Babe. During the 1920s, Babe's New York Yankees were the most powerful team in baseball. In fact, many people think the 1927 Yankees were the greatest team ever. Led by Ruth and first baseman Lou "The Iron Horse" Gehrig, the Yanks won the American League pennant by 19 games. To follow that up, in the World Series they swept the Pittsburgh Pirates in four straight games. The Yankee lineup was nicknamed Murderers' Row. And for good reason: the *team* batting average that year was a whopping .307!

THE WORLD'S CHAMPION

ONE PACKED IN EACH BOX OF

BUBBLE GUM

He waves his cap to the huge calling-out.

He loves this moment.

He is theirs.

They are his.

He is the Babe.

And he has changed baseball.

Forever.

— No. 264 —

🙠 THE SLOW TROT HOME—
AGAIN AND AGAIN! 🙢

Babe's 714 major league home run record stood for almost 40 years. But to understand how Babe ruled the baseball world of his time, think of this: when he retired in 1935 with 714 homers, he had *more than twice as many* as any other player in the game! The home run, as one writer put it, "belonged to him." Or, as another sportswriter wrote after one of Babe's game-winning grand slams, "It was Ruth, the whole Ruth, and nothing but the Ruth."

THE WORLD'S CHAMPION

ONE PACKED IN EACH BOX OF

BUBBLE GUM

*For my father—who loved
the game
—R. B.*

*For my son, Eli,
to help him learn the spirit of can-do
—M. W.*

Text copyright © 1998 by Robert Burleigh
Illustrations copyright © 1998 by Mike Wimmer

www.HarcourtBooks.com

First Voyager Books edition 2003
Voyager Books is a trademark of Harcourt, Inc.,
registered in the United States of America and/or other jurisdictions.

The Library of Congress has cataloged the hardcover edition as follows:
Burleigh, Robert.
Home run: the story of Babe Ruth/Robert Burleigh;
illustrated by Mike Wimmer.
p. cm.
Summary: A poetic account of the legendary Babe Ruth as he prepares to hit a home run.
1. Ruth, Babe, 1895–1948—Juvenile fiction. [1. Ruth, Babe, 1895–1948—Fiction.
2. Baseball—Fiction.] I. Wimmer, Mike, ill. II. Title.
PZ7.B9244Ho   1998
[E]—dc20   95-10038
ISBN 0-15-200970-1
ISBN 0-15-204599-6 pb

A C E G H F D B

The illustrations in this book were done in oils on canvas.
The display type was hand-lettered by Tom Seibert.
The text type was set in Garamond #3 by Thompson Type, San Diego, California.
Color separations by United Graphic Pte. Ltd., Singapore
Printed and bound by Tien Wah Press, Singapore
Production supervision by Sandra Grebenar and Wendi Taylor
Designed by Lisa Peters